SARAJEVO

SARAJEVO

A PORTRAIT OF THE SIEGE

PRODUCED BY MATTHEW NAYTHONS
PICTURE SELECTION AND DESIGN BY ALEX CASTRO
TEXT EDITED BY REBECCA BUFFUM TAYLOR

AN EPICENTER COMMUNICATIONS BOOK

WARNER BOOKS, INC.
A TIME WARNER COMPANY

To the men, women, and children of Sarajevo.

Created and Produced by
Epicenter Communications
Sausalito, California 94965

Epicenter Communications:
    President: Matthew Naythons
    VP, Executive Editor: Rebecca Buffum Taylor
    VP, Art Director: Alex Castro
    Project Manager: Dawn Sheggeby
    Assistant Editor: Kate Warne
    Administrative Assistant: Erika Gulick Smith
Also for Epicenter:
    Director of Photographic Research:
        Marcel Saba, Saba Press Photos
    Photo Researcher: Evan Nisselson, Saba Press Photos
    Caption Writer: Michael Tharp
    Editorial Adviser: Dean Toda
    Photo research in Sarajevo: Suzanne Keating

Warner Books, Inc.
Time & Life Building
1271 Avenue of the Americas
New York, New York 10020

A Time Warner Company

Printed in Italy
First Printing: March 1994
10 9 8 7 6 5 4 3 2 1

ISBN: 0-446-51824-7
LC: 93-61175

Previous pages: As the twentieth
century dawned, Lombardy poplars
and the meandering Miljacka River
provided a peaceful backdrop for the
most picturesque city in the Balkans;
a pre–World War I view of City Hall
and the Imperial Bridge in the heart
of Sarajevo.

Ethnographisches Museum

This page: Sarajevans stroll along the
river in front of the Academy of Arts
building near the National Theater
before the siege.

Anto Jelavic

PROLOGUE

From the shores of my peace, luck, games, and satisfaction, someone with a horrible force of war, which I am terrified of, is trying to pull me, and pull me away. I feel like a swimmer who doesn't want to jump into hot water, but is forced to do so. I feel surprised, sad, and scared, and ask myself, where is it that they are pushing me? I ask myself why they stole the peaceful shore of my childhood. I used to look forward to every new day, for each single day was beautiful in its own way. I looked forward to the sun, games, songs—I enjoyed my childhood. I did not need anything more.

I try to understand all of this, but I can't. Sometimes I believe it is all a bad dream, and with all my strength I try to wake up.

When I look through my shattered window, I see a completely different picture than when the window was in one piece. I realize again that I am not dreaming.

There are no trees; people have cut them down to survive through the winter. I see people who are lucky or maybe unlucky to stay alive. Everyone has been tortured, and many have become invalids without hands or legs. They are joined by the children, who in reality aren't children anymore. Each has had his or her childhood stolen, and there can be no children without childhoods. They are now little big people. They recognize death and horror, and know that everything has been stolen from them, even the animals. All of the animals in the zoo have been killed. There are few dogs, cats, or even pigeons—the symbol of Sarajevo. Household pets are dying, because their owners have no food to feed them. Everything is dead or will soon die.

The power of war destroys everything. Slowly, a city is disappearing.

With the help of my parents, good books, a piano, my good friend Mirna, and my great neighbors, I try not to think about what I see, hear, and feel.

So put me back on the shore of my childhood. There I was happy and satisfied. There it was warm.

Zlata Filipovic, a 12-year-old Sarajevan girl,
translated by Edin Lemes

Middle-class Sarajevans stand in a breadline. During the siege, the minimum wait was often two hours for a single 10-ounce loaf.
Tom Stoddart

1389	Serbia is defeated by Muslim Turks in the Battle of Kosovo, setting the stage for four centuries of Turkish rule and Serbian resentment of Muslims.
1463	Bosnia comes under rule by Muslim Turks.
1878	Serbia achieves independence from the faltering Ottoman Empire. The Austro-Hungarian Empire wrests control of Bosnia and Herzegovina, and Serbs, who make up a third of Bosnia-Herzegovina's people, agitate for Austrian withdrawal and union with Serbia—the root of Serbian nationalism in Bosnia.
1912–13	Serbia, Bulgaria, and Greece ally to force the Turks from their last European bastions of Thrace and Macedonia in the First Balkan War; the Second Balkan War follows as the three countries turn on each other in a bitter nationalistic struggle to control the liberated territory. Bosnia is involved in neither war.
1914–18	In Sarajevo, Serbian nationalist Gavrilo Princip assassinates Archduke Ferdinand of Austria. A complex web of European alliances leads the ensuing conflict between Austria and Serbia to escalate into World War I. Territorial settlements at the close of the war create Yugoslavia from eight provinces and independent countries, including Serbia, Croatia, and Bosnia.
1939–45	Tempted by Nazi promises of a "Greater Croatia" during World War II, Croatian Fascists collaborate with the invading Germans and kill hundreds of thousands of Serbs; Serbian Chetniks in turn massacre Croatian civilians as well as Bosnian Muslims.
1945–80	Josip Broz, a Croatian Communist resistance leader known by the nom de guerre Tito, comes to power in Yugoslavia. He keeps the peace domestically with a no-tolerance policy toward ethnic nationalism and with official steps to reduce the power of Serbs, the country's largest ethnic group.
1980–90	Tito dies. Yugoslavia is ruled by a collective presidency, made up of one representative from each of its eight regions. The relatively stable multiethnic country hosts the 1984 Winter Olympics in Sarajevo.
1990	Three nationalist leaders come to power within the Yugoslavian federation in a shift toward increasing ethnic consciousness among Yugoslavs. Alija Izetbegovic is elected Bosnia's president by Muslim nationalists. After an anti-Serb, pro-independence campaign, Franjo Tudjman, a longtime Croatian nationalist, is elected Croatia's president. And under the rise of nationalist Slobodan Milosevic, once an old-line Communist, Serbia annexes the autonomous provinces of Vojvodina and Kosovo.

Gavrilo Princip, the young Bosnian Serb who changed history by igniting the Great War, shot Austria's Archduke Franz Ferdinand from this street corner in Sarajevo. Footprints in the paving stone memorialized his success until they were smashed during the siege; across the street, Princip Bridge stands as a reminder of World War I, also fought for a "Greater Serbia."
Truman Moore

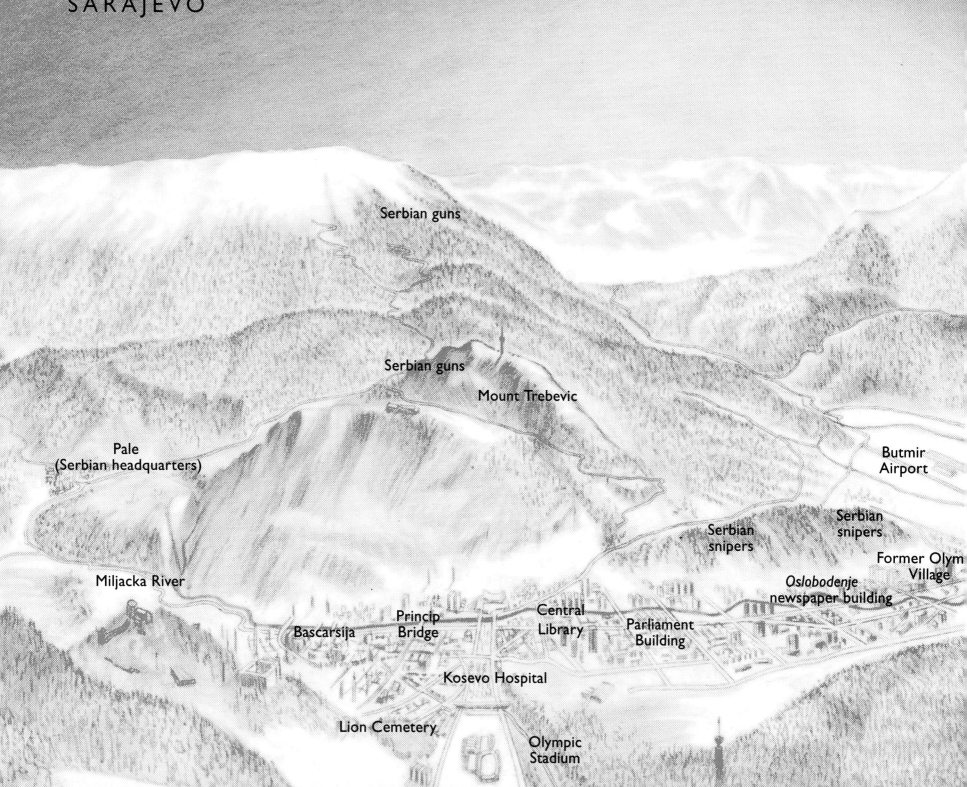

SARAJEVO

Serbian guns

Serbian guns

Mount Trebevic

Pale
(Serbian headquarters)

Butmir
Airport

Serbian
snipers

Serbian
snipers

Former Olym
Village

Miljacka River

Oslobodenje
newspaper building

Princip
Bridge

Central
Library

Parliament
Building

Bascarsija

Kosevo Hospital

Lion Cemetery

Olympic
Stadium

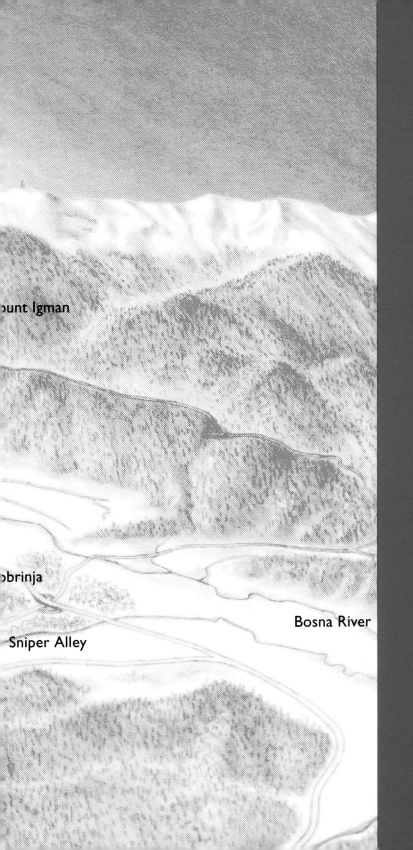

Mount Igman

Dobrinja

Bosna River

Sniper Alley

| May 15, 1991 | Controlling half of the votes in the collective presidency, the pro-Serb faction—Serbia, its annexed provinces, and its ally Montenegro—unconstitutionally blocks Croatian Stipe Mesic's rotation into the chairmanship, leaving Yugoslavia without a head of state. |

| June 25, 1991 | Embittered by Serbia's increasing control of Yugoslavia, Croatia and Slovenia proclaim their independence. Ethnic Serbs in both regions fight to keep their districts formally tied to the Yugoslav federation. |

| August 25, 1991 | Dropping its pretense of neutrality, the Serb-dominated Yugoslav National Army comes to the aid of Serbian rebels in Croatia. Germany retaliates by recognizing the independence of Croatia, its ally in World War II, which spurs Serbian leaders to unveil a blueprint for redividing Yugoslavia along ethnic lines. |

| September 25, 1991 | In its first direct involvement in the conflict, the UN imposes an arms embargo on Yugoslavia, banning delivery of all weapons or military equipment. |

| December 20, 1991 | Bosnia's president, Izetbegovic, asks the UN for troops to prevent fighting in Serbia and Croatia from spreading to Bosnia, trapped between the two provinces. |

| January 3, 1992 | A cease-fire agreement in Croatia—the 15th mediated cease-fire of the Yugoslavian conflict—succeeds in maintaining peace, freeing Serbian forces to devote their resources to the Serbs fighting in Bosnia. |

| February 29–March 1, 1992 | Ethnic Croats and Muslims in Bosnia vote overwhelmingly for Bosnia to break from Yugoslavia, declaring their faith in multiethnic democracy. Many Bosnian Serbs boycott the election, and within weeks fight to block Bosnia's independence, afraid their rights would be diminished under Muslim leadership. |

| March–April 1992 | Several more cease-fires arranged by European Community (EC) and UN mediators raise hopes of a quick end to the Bosnian conflict, but none lasts more than a few days. In April, Serbs position mortars, artillery, and snipers in the hills around Sarajevo, laying siege to the political and spiritual capital of Bosnia. |

| May 1992 | Both the EC and the UN impose heavy trade sanctions on Yugoslavia, which now consists only of Serbia and Montenegro; Serbs retaliate by fiercely shelling Sarajevo. The Yugoslav National Army frees 55,000 Bosnian Serbs—well-armed, well-trained soldiers—to serve in the Bosnian Serb Army. |

| June 29, 1992 | A small UN contingent opens the Sarajevo airport for relief supplies after it had been closed for 87 days. Within weeks, the UN sends 500 additional troops to keep the airport open, by force if necessary. |

August 4, 1992	Reports of gruesome mistreatment of Muslim and Croatian civilians lead the UN to demand access to detention camps in Serb-held Bosnia. The UN Security Council later condemns Serbia's policy of "ethnic cleansing" of non-Serbs.
August 26–27, 1992	The London Peace Conference, the war's first international peace effort, is attended by leaders of all factions in Bosnia. The talks, sponsored by the EC and the UN, call for an end to violence in Bosnia, an end to the siege of Sarajevo, and a schedule of continued peace talks in Geneva.
October 27, 1992	Cyrus Vance of the UN and Lord David Owen of the EC introduce a plan to divide Bosnia into 10 semiautonomous multiethnic regions, which would leave Sarajevo an "open city" not under the control of any one ethnic group.
November 16, 1992	After two days of debate, the UN decides not to exempt Bosnia from the arms embargo, despite the severe disparity in weapons favoring the Serbs.
December 20, 1992	With temperatures near zero, sporadic electricity, and lack of heating fuel, the first deaths from freezing are reported in Sarajevo.
January 2, 1993	At peace talks in Geneva, leaders of the Bosnian Croats and Muslims voice support for the Vance-Owen plan, but Bosnian Serbs, now in control of 70% of Bosnian territory, continue to hold out for their own ethnic state.
May 15, 1993	Bosnian Serb voters emphatically reject the Vance-Owen peace plan, a move seen as its death knell. The UN settles on a plan for Muslim "safe havens," including Sarajevo, but Bosnia's Izetbegovic denounces them as "ghettoes."
June 21, 1993	At a new round of Geneva peace talks, Serbian and Croatian leaders suggest splitting Bosnia into three ethnically homogeneous regions; Muslims remain opposed, as it would leave them with little land and no access to the sea.
June 27, 1993	The UN halves its food distribution efforts in Bosnia, citing a drop in donations and the difficulty of keeping convoys safe.
July 26, 1993	Serbian fighters gain control of Igman and Bjelasnica, two strategic mountains overlooking Sarajevo—and controlling a tenuous route Muslims had used to smuggle arms and goods into the city. Two weeks later, in response to NATO and UN threats, Serbs agree to pull back from the peaks if they are replaced by UN troops.
September 1, 1993	The second peace plan, which proposed partitioning Bosnia into three regions along ethnic lines, is rejected by Muslim leaders, wary of the other two regions' potential for joining with the states of Serbia and Croatia.

Previous pages: A presiege view from above Sarajevo's Old Town, with City Hall just below the minaret.

Jerry Cooke

A contemporary view of an Orthodox Christian Church, home to religious Serbs, contrasts an historic view of the Gazi Husref Beg Mosque, built by Muslims in 1530 and widely regarded as the most imposing mosque in the Balkans. An inscription in the mosque's forecourt proved to be tragically prophetic: "Husref Beg was overtaken by darkness in a state which was not sleep."

Left: Patrice Habans
Right: Ethnographisches Museum

Night falls on a peaceful Sarajevo before the siege. Most residents saw themselves first and foremost as Sarajevans, not as Muslims, Serbs, Croats, or Jews. Their harmony, combined with President Tito's nonaligned foreign policy, contributed to Yugoslavia's post–World War II stability.

Michael Hayman

Bascarsija, Sarajevo's ancient Turkish bazaar and the oldest part of the city, was a warren of hundreds of tiny shops and wooden stalls for merchants and coppersmiths before the siege. A guidebook describes the market as "a noisy, smoky, hectic place"; here a craftsman works late into the night after the crowds have gone home.

Gianni Berengo Gardin

Four years after Tito's death, Yugoslavia holds together to host the 1984 Winter Olympics in Sarajevo, watched over by Tito's likeness and legacy on the boulevard that still bears his name. A nearby eternal flame honored Tito and his partisans, the city's World War II liberators, until it was extinguished by officials during the siege when residents, their electric power cut off, began using it for cooking. *At right:* Flags from competing nations along the promenade in front of the Olympic Center.

Left: Bill Bachman
Right: Anto Jelavic

Benjamin and Miroslav were friends. Benjamin was a Muslim filmmaker, Miroslav a Croatian engineering student at Sarajevo University.

When I first met them in May 1990, they introduced me to a third friend, Branko, a Serb. They had all grown up in Sarajevo and "could talk about anything to each other," Benjamin said.

"The people of Bosnia have learned, through enormous suffering, how to get along," Miroslav added.

I drove around Sarajevo with Benjamin and Miroslav in Benjamin's tiny car, navigating the hills above the town and talking about Bosnians.

That is, whether they existed.

Miroslav and Benjamin called themselves Bosnians. But what was a Bosnian? Was there some distinctive quality that all inhabitants of Bosnia—Serb, Croat, and Muslim—shared? They groped for a way to explain it to me. "It's a feeling," Miroslav said. "A philosophy of life."

Benjamin rubbed his fingertips together, caressing the gossamer-thin nuance of Bosnianness. "A certain outlook."

"Exactly." Miroslav said. "A unique outlook formed by the fact that the different groups live so close to each other."

"Yes, our differences are what we have in common," Benjamin concluded triumphantly, happy to have formulated this paradox, this bon mot.

We stopped at a hillside *kafana*—a traditional coffee shop—with windows framing a view of Sarajevo in the valley below and snow-capped mountains beyond. We sat on the cushioned benches running along the walls and drank our coffee from little porcelain cups. We dipped our sugar cubes in the coffee and sucked on them, Bosnian-style.

Benjamin was gazing out the window, down on the city. "There is a place in Sarajevo," he said, "where an Orthodox church, a Catholic church, a mosque, and a synagogue all stand within 50 meters of one another. There is no trouble between them. Isn't that amazing? That's what Bosnia is all about."

I, too, looked over the minarets, the steeples, the domes. I could pick out the corner where the Archduke Franz Ferdinand was shot and World War I began. "Zagreb is like the brain of Yugoslavia," Miroslav was saying. "Universities, rationality, and so on. Belgrade is the heart. Passion, anger. But Sarajevo! Sarajevo is the soul."

The designation seemed appropriate. While Belgrade thundered and Zagreb panicked, Sarajevo brooded. The brain and heart could be held in the hand, weighed. The soul was the most exalted of the three, but many people did not believe it existed.

Miroslav and Benjamin went on talking, arguing excitedly that Bosnia had a chance to play an historic role in reconciling the nations of Yugoslavia. But I could not help noticing that although Branko was their good Serbian friend, I had seen very little of him.

Brian Hall, author of *The Impossible Country*

Before the siege, a craftsman and his friend sit in front of his shop in the Bascarsija section of the city. Their traditional *dzeva* coffee set was made from copper by the craftsman.
James Mason

Following pages: **Four centuries of Ottoman rule are reflected in a presiege view of a Turkish cemetery on the city's outskirts, its nobles' tombstones capped with turbans. Minarets piercing the sky from dozens of mosques further show Islam's lasting influence more than a century after the Ottoman occupation ended.**
Truman Moore

Participants in a peace demonstration involving some 400 Sarajevans—Muslims, Croats, and Serbs—on April 5, 1992, these men display an old Yugoslav flag as a symbol of mutual coexistence. The next day, when Bosnia's independence from the Yugoslav federation was formally proclaimed, their ranks swelled to nearly 200,000 as they demanded civilian control of the former Yugoslav army.

Ron Haviv

Their idealism shattered, the demonstrators take cover from Serbian snipers firing from the windows of the nearby Holiday Inn. The dying words of Suada Dilberović a young woman from Dubrovnik, Croatia, who became the first casualty of the siege, are said to have been: "Oh, please do not tell me this is happening in Sarajevo."

Ron Haviv

In a scene that would become familiar to all Sarajevans, an artillery shell explodes in a downtown parking lot a month after the siege begins. Rounds would fall at any time and in any place throughout the city, and the randomness of the deadly hail drove many Sarajevans to the outer edges of sanity.

Andrew Reid

Residents searching for bodies, food, and medicine dig through the debris of a Red Cross convoy after it was attacked in May 1992. It soon became clear that no one—civilian or soldier, adult or child, relief worker or peacekeeper—was immune from Serbian gunners.

Peter Northall

A volunteer at a first-aid center identifies a Bosnian civilian killed by mortar fire. In the early weeks of the siege, Olympic sites, public auditoriums, and theaters became makeshift hospitals and morgues. Since World War II, all Sarajevan adults have carried an identity card.

Peter Northall

Although its building was burned to the ground, the daily paper *Oslobodenje*—meaning "freedom"—continued to print a few thousand copies each day on basement presses. This headline, reminiscent of the memorial to the man who shot Archduke Ferdinand and ignited World War I, reads: "Bloody Footprints of Crime."

David Brauchli

Two of the city's tallest buildings burn in the spring of 1992 after being hit by artillery rounds. Sarajevans came to display an extraordinary ability to carry on life's ordinary ceremonies and rituals: some white-collar workers continued to report to work each day in this building after the shelling.

Steve Connors

A portrait of the Old Man of Yugoslavia lies in the ruins of an abandoned building. Graffiti appeared early in the siege: "Tito, come back! All is forgiven." Scrawled beneath it: "No chance. —Tito."

Andrew Reid

Her own home leveled, Antonia
Arapovic finds shelter in the
basement of a nearby house during
a mortar attack; later, as the shelling
continues, she tries to comfort her
neighbor's son. As Slavenka Drakulic,
a Croatian journalist and novelist,
once wrote: "War is not a single act,
it is a state of facts and minds, a
head-spinning spiral of events and
a gradual process of realization."

Tom Stoddart

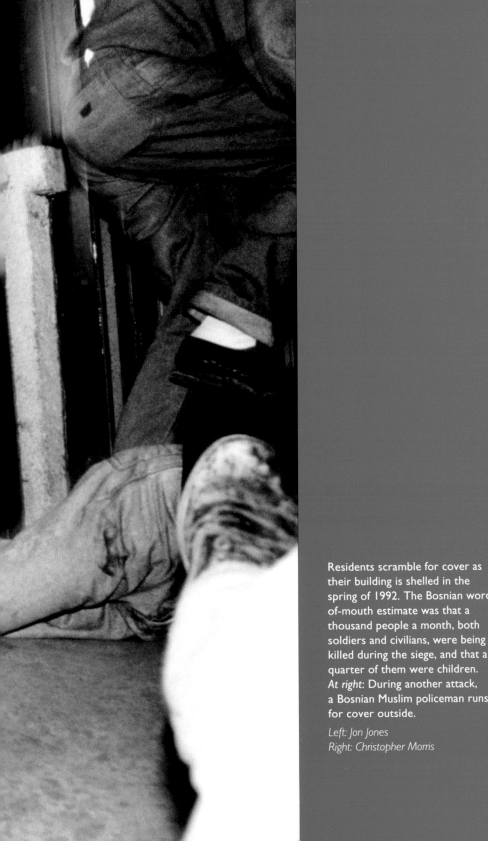

Residents scramble for cover as their building is shelled in the spring of 1992. The Bosnian word-of-mouth estimate was that a thousand people a month, both soldiers and civilians, were being killed during the siege, and that a quarter of them were children. *At right*: During another attack, a Bosnian Muslim policeman runs for cover outside.

Left: Jon Jones
Right: Christopher Morris

Moments after his home was destroyed, a man saves what he can from the wreckage, risking sniper fire to carry a few precious heirlooms to a safer place.

Christopher Morris

Following pages: A Muslim sniper peers warily through a shell hole. As the siege dragged on, all sides came to rely on sniper fire as an unwritten rule of engagement.

Patrick Chauvel

Everyone in Sarajevo remembers his last normal day: "It was June 16, 1992; I remember because my husband and I took the baby for a walk in his stroller, and the local newspaper took our photograph," says my friend Klea, who is 24 and married to a computer expert turned soldier. She still has that photograph. When she has not left her tiny two-room house for a week because of the heavy shelling, and when the baby has not stopped crying because he is hungry and cold, she takes that photograph out of the drawer and stares at it. "To remember who I was."

Small touches left behind show that a normal world once existed. One day I found a tourist map of Sarajevo printed shortly after the 1984 Winter Olympics. The sort of map you get for free when you rent a car, it lists the neighborhoods that are now front lines; bus routes that no longer exist; abandoned ski lifts; boarded-up restaurants; and three-star hotels, now unheated, unlit, and full of refugees. It was printed in bright colors and says this: "In 13 museums and archives there lives the past of this city; the history of the life together of Muslims, Serbs, Croats, Jews, and other nationalities of Yugoslavia, who have lived here for centuries and intend to continue so."

One cold day I pored over that map with Klea's father, Mario Susko, a former professor of English from Sarajevo University. Mario chain-smoked, stamped his feet for warmth, and told me that before the siege his life meant translating Saul Bellow and e. e. cummings into Serbo-Croatian. Then, he lived with his wife, Maria, a former dental technician, and their other daughter, 16-year-old Alexandra, in a beautiful apartment in Dobrinja, a 10-minute drive from my hotel down Sniper Alley. Originally built as housing for the Olympic athletes, the apartments in Dobrinja were sold to middle-class families who wanted a bit of space, good schools for their children, and some grass to sit on in the summer. Now Dobrinja is one of the most dangerous frontline neighborhoods in Sarajevo, and there are neat rows of makeshift graves in front of the apartment blocks because it is too dangerous to bring the dead into the central city.

Some days Mario is too afraid to leave the house at all. "You can kill life without actually killing everyone," he says. "It's a psychological way to destroy the civilian population by taking away, bit by bit, our normal life."

Janine di Giovanni, *The Sunday Times* of London

Sarajevans run for cover across an intersection to avoid sniper fire. A young businessman who eventually escaped Sarajevo described the simple act of crossing a street: "You feel as if you are exposed on a plate, and you always look for a doorway to hide in." Since snipers moved their positions almost hourly, the wisdom of survival became simple: if you can see the hills, the hills can see you.

Tom Stoddart

A Bosnian Muslim militiaman tries
to force open a door as he searches
house to house for weapons left
behind by Serbs. While most sniper
fire came from the hills surrounding
Sarajevo, some Serbian snipers—
reviled by residents as "fifth
columnists"—operated within the
city. The UN arms embargo on
Bosnia left the Muslims significantly
underarmed and dependent on
scavenging for weapons.

Christopher Morris

Passersby help a man who was shot
in the head by a sniper while driving.

Patrick Chauvel

Following pages: Blood and bits of
clothing are all that remain after
22 bodies were removed from the
bakery storefront where the
victims, killed by Serbian gunners
on May 27, 1992, had been
standing in line for bread.

Peter Northall

In spite of the horrors in the abandoned city, local writer Abdulah Sidran has said, "It is a privilege to be Sarajevan." Despite the prolonged siege and daily loss of lives, our basic values are preserved, and Sarajevo is still a place where a good song can be composed, where Beckett's *Godot* can still be staged.

There is no Sarajevo story that has not been told, except perhaps the unknown stories of ordinary citizens and their daily lives. There are two things an average Sarajevan cares about: to save his life and to preserve his dignity. While Karadzic engages His Lordship David Owen to assist in his mapmaking business, Sarajevan Muslims, Serbs, Croats, Jews, and others wait in a long queue for water. The people whose lives are most affected by various partition plans are trapped so tightly and cut off so efficiently that they don't even have batteries for their radios to hear news from Geneva. We can print only 3,000 copies of *Oslobodenje*, Sarajevo's daily paper, for our 300,000 citizens because of the lack of printing paper and oil to run the press generator.

The background of the Geneva talks on Bosnia is a very Serbian idea that "the common life is not possible." And at the same time, Sarajevo is havng its love affair of forbidden common life. But precisely because of this Sarajevan stubbornness in believing in multiethnicity and multinationality, the city is condemned to death.

It is a strange and unique siege that lets the best people of the world come in and the worst among them decide over citizens' destinies. Whoever will be looked after by the UN in the future will be forewarned by the Bosnian experience.

The last television crew to visit us at *Oslobodenje* asked me what I think of Europe. My instant answer: it is not polite to ask a Sarajevan about Europe; but since it was an Australian journalist interviewing me in front of the ruined *Oslobodenje* building, I simply told him, "This is Europe. You are now in Europe." Only later did I wonder whether Europe is the ruin around me or some other, peaceful place, where people go on holiday.

Nobody can write a letter to a Sarajevan address. Nobody can phone to a Sarajevan friend. Few Sarajevans can send a simple message. It was Susan Sontag who, sitting in a Sarajevo shelter, said, "This was a short century. It started in Sarajevo in 1914, and it ended in Sarajevo in 1992."

The privilege of being Sarajevan is to do something with the end of the century. You do not pity yourself for not being able to join the next one.

Gordana Knezevic, editor, *Oslobodenje*

As a requiem to those killed in the breadline, cellist Vedran Smailovic plays Albinoni's "Adagio" at the site of the attack. Risking sniper fire himself while he played, Smailovic, a member of the Sarajevo Opera orchestra, repeated his tribute for 22 consecutive days.

Andrew Reid

After several knocks, the door opened a crack. The face peering anxiously into the darkened corridor was that of a 40-year-old Serbian teacher, one of thousands of Serbs still living in Sarajevo after months under siege by Serbian nationalist troops. The man was ashen-faced, so fearful that his hands trembled.

"Forgive me, I am not myself," he said, after ushering his guest in and taking a few moments to compose himself. "We feel incarcerated here. We sit here languishing, afraid to go out, terrified that there will be a knock on the door from armed men who will drag me out, take me to the mountains and make me dig trenches or fight against my own people."

Life in the Bosnian capital is full of hunger and spiraling misery . . . and there is less talk of hope that Sarajevo will rise from the ruins after the war. Instead, there is a growing sense that there may be no future here for Serbs, at least none for Serbs wishing to live as equals with Muslims and Croats.

"Just walking down the street these days, you feel something at the back of your neck," said a Serbian engineer, one of many Serbs who agreed to be interviewed on condition that they not be named.

"There is still something left of the old life here," he added, "Muslim friends from years ago whom you can rely on, people with whom you can ignore everything that's happened. But there are a lot of Muslim refugees, people who have been the victims of 'ethnic cleansing,' and for them, the Serb represents everything that is hateful."

Most Serbs who were interviewed said that they could not accept a view that put the Serbian nationalists on an equal moral plane with the Muslim leaders. A college professor, preparing to try to escape the city, said that he had thought often of Muslims as he struggled to pack the suitcase he planned to take with him.

"I spend my time packing and unpacking, picking and choosing between all the things I love, my old books and my family souvenirs, old birthday gifts, knowing that I have time to take what I value most, and say goodbye to the rest," the man said. "Then I think of Muslims who were victims of 'ethnic cleansing,' being given five minutes to pack a nylon bag, and being kicked out of their homes forever, at the point of a gun. That is something I can never understand, and never forgive."

John F. Burns, *The New York Times*

In the suburb of Dobrinja, a Bosnian civilian prepares to defend his home against a Serbian assault. Dobrinja had been a quiet, residential area where inter-marriages among Serbs, Croats, and Muslims were common. Eventually most city streets became war zones, as Sarajevans from all backgrounds fought together to save their city from the Serbian nationalists in the hills.

Andrew Reid

Using the cramped trunk of a car as a makeshift ambulance, a father cradles his wounded child. As casualties mounted, grief became a constant—and growing—burden on Sarajevans.

Antoine Gyori

His semiautomatic weapon readied, a Muslim man covers firemen as they try to quench a blaze across the street, an effort abandoned as this Serbian attack intensified.

Christopher Morris

A field dressing taped hastily to his wound, a soldier is propelled by a comrade toward temporary cover. Helmets and flak jackets, invaluable protection, were in scant supply; and as the siege dragged on, injured soldiers were pressed back into defending the city.

Antoine Gyori

Early in the siege, Croats edge around a corner while civilians stand by. Muslims made up the bulk of the city's defenders, but Croats and even Serbian residents took up arms against their attackers.

Andrew Reid

A Serbian sniper steadies his rifle and peers through a high-powered scope, searching for targets in a Sarajevo neighborhood. It was widely rumored that Serbian snipers were paid bounties not only for shooting journalists and political officials, but also for shooting children—one of the more horrific methods of "ethnic cleansing."

Art Zamur

On June 29, 1992, nearly three months after the bombardment of Sarajevo began and the airport was closed, French and Canadian UN troops reopen the runways and control tower. Up to 15 relief-flight pilots, together carrying 250 tons of aid, immediately began risking Serbian fire to land each day.

James Mason

The first UN Protection Force, or UNPROFOR, convoy to reach the besieged suburb of Dobrinja appears in early July 1992. UN soldiers, hamstrung by restrictive rules on how to carry out their mission of protecting civilians and relief convoys, frequently came under fire themselves; but cynical Sarajevans, frustrated by the quality of "protection" they received, began calling the UN force "SERBPROFOR."

Left: Tom Stoddart
Right: Antoine Gyori

met Tomislav Jozic, a priest, on a sweltering afternoon in July of 1992. He was leaning out of the door of the Catholic charity Caritas, scolding a crowd who had gathered to collect food. The wait, he tried to convince them, would be futile. During the first week of the airlift, Jozic had received only 614 parcels to distribute among his district's 9,000 residents. He ran out within two days, but hungry people still queued outside his door as early as five in the morning. Three months into the siege, Jozic was exasperated by the conflicting demands he felt as a priest, as an unwilling public-welfare official, and as a hungry, humiliated Sarajevan. Only days earlier, armed representatives of the Territorial Defense Force had accused him of distributing aid only to the district's Croats. Jozic angrily flipped open a brown ledger on his desk, jabbing at a list of recipients' names. "They are Serbs, Muslims, and Croats," he scowled. "Anybody who queues will get food as long as it is here." Jozic was wildly offended by the insinuation that he was sympathetic to the tribalist politics tearing apart his city. Ethnic affiliation was far less important than whether someone belonged to the "hill people"—the nationalist extremists pulverizing the city from the hills above, or to the "city people"—the beleaguered Serbs, Muslims, and Croats all trying to survive on the ground below.

And like most Sarajevo survivors, Jozic had already become a bitter pragmatist. When a sniper fired on a parish priest on his way to conduct a funeral, Jozic decided that from then on, parishioners killed in unsafe neighborhoods would be buried without a priest present. He relied on neighbors and soldiers to keep him apprised of those who died. "There have been so many funerals," he said, "I can no longer count them." He could remember only one wedding since the siege began, in late April.

Jozic finally started telling parishioners not to come to mass. "If there is a crowded church on Sunday, we are a perfect target," he said matter-of-factly. "It's my moral obligation to protect them." When a handful of people kept showing up anyway, Jozic conducted what he described with a chuckle as an "express mass," afterward sending people out of the church a few at a time, so that gunners in the hills above couldn't fix their sights on a crowd. The length of the service, said Jozic, was "a military secret. If I tell you when it begins, they can figure out when people will be leaving."

And what does a priest tell people about God and faith when their lives are being destroyed? "I try to tell them something about hope," he finally answered after a long pause. "Hope is the last thing to die."

Karen Breslau, *Newsweek*

Eyes closed to the madness, a woman recoils moments after witnessing a mortar attack—which left six people dead and dozens wounded—near the city center.

Luc Delahaye

Ruza Glavas, the grandmother of a child killed by sniper fire, is carried from her grandchild's funeral—wounded herself—seconds after a mortar round exploded in the cemetery. BBC correspondent Kevin Connolly (nearest camera) and Reuter correspondent Kurt Schork (with glasses) move the woman to safety.

Corinne Dufka

Sarajevans comfort one another at a funeral. Bereaved residents continued to perform their ceremonies for the dead, although Serbian gunners became notorious for targeting burial sites.

Christopher Morris

A Muslim defender's family anguishes at his graveside after he was killed by a grenade on October 7, 1992. In one of the deadliest days of the siege to that date, 11 others were killed and 88 wounded.

Corinne Dufka

Kneeling amid freshly dug graves, Orthodox Christian mourners silently recite funeral prayers. Graves were marked with crosses for Christians and six-sided wooden boards for Muslims; headstones for Communists and atheists were marked with stars.

Jon Jones

A young man wounded by sniper fire is comforted by a friend. The attack had come while the man was attending the funeral of his brother.
Luigi Baldelli

Sarajevans sprint past their dead and wounded neighbors during a mortar attack along Marshal Tito Boulevard. A segment of the city's main avenue, exposed to nearby hills, became known—grimly—as Sniper Alley.
Luc Delahaye

Biljana Vhrovac, a 20-year-old Serb, struggles to rise after seeing her father (behind her) and her dog killed and losing an arm during a noonday mortar attack. Residents came to fear mortars even more than artillery: fired from much closer range, mortars possessed a deadly accuracy.

Luc Delahaye

A woman, trying to negotiate a rubble-strewn street in high heels, sprints for cover during a Serbian attack. Despite the constant danger of falling rounds, many Sarajevans wore their usual workday clothes to preserve a sense of normalcy amid the violence around them.

Tom Haley

*S*arajevo became a point of refuge for women raped in smaller, nearby towns, a "safe haven" that held at least the hope of medical care and protection.

In May 1992, Serbs took Ilijas, a town near Sarajevo. A number of Muslims stayed on to protect their homes, including Mulija Bersa, a registered nurse, and Dzemal, her husband, the head of a local union. In July 1992, when she was nine months pregnant, Mulija was visited by Serbian militiamen and a family friend.

My husband had been this friend's witness at his wedding. In the house with me were my husband, our 16-year-old niece, and my mother-in-law. When the whole family was gathered, the militiamen cut the throat of my mother-in-law. Forcing us to watch, three of them abused our niece, raped her, and then cut her throat, too.

My husband kept begging his former friend to let me go to the hospital. Instead, they separated us. [Weeks later Mulija would find out that Dzemal's throat had been cut and his body dumped in a river.]

I was brought to a jail near Café Sonja, a motel where Serbian fighters come to rape and kill Muslim women. First they brutalized me, then put me in a room where I was abused, tortured, and raped. I lost consciousness a couple of times. I was bleeding. One of them, Borislav Herak, after raping me, took me to another room where he showed me a great number of commando knives. He asked me to "pick the knife you want me to kill you with." I resisted. He beat on me again and again, and it never seemed to end. He hit me with his fists and the butt of his gun, punching my belly many times. Exhausted, I picked up a knife. Then he asked me, "Do you want me to abort you from your belly or from your vagina?"

Other people were present, laughing, having a good time. It is in this room that I witnessed a 13-year-old girl being raped over and over. At one point a Serbian militiaman whom I used to know from the hospital came in. He purposely left the door open. I escaped from Café Sonja, crawling on my knees. On the grass outside, I gave birth to my little girl, Almira. I fainted. When I came back to my senses, an older Muslim woman was helping me. She cut the umbilical cord and took care of the baby. Later she brought us to a Bosnian Muslim checkpoint in Sarajevo, where we were sent to Kosevo Hospital.

Almira had many bruises, many black-and-blue marks from the blows I had received. She was placed in an incubator with four other babies while I was operated on twice. A few days later, the Serbs shelled the nursery. Bombs were falling all around us. I left my room holding my perfusion equipment and ran upstairs to get my daughter. When I arrived in the room, of the five babies in the incubators, only one was alive. It was Almira.

Mulija Bersa, as told to Frank Fournier,
with interpreter Sabina Arslanajic

Borislav Herak, a 22-year-old Bosnian Serb from Sarajevo, awaits trial in the city's Viktor Buban military prison. His case crystallized international outrage against the war's brutal crimes against women: the EC estimated that 20,000 Muslims had been raped by Serbs by the winter of 1993. Herak was eventually sentenced to death, convicted of 16 rapes and 35 murders; in sum, he had participated in or witnessed more than 200 rapes and murders. Herak was also one of the first men slated to be tried by the UN-initiated War Crimes Court, the first of its kind since the Nuremberg trials after World War II.

Frank Fournier

Like a morning haze, a deceptive calm hangs over the city. Centuries earlier, Turks had named the capital of their western territories Saraj Ovasi, "the field of palaces," but almost daily bombardment marred most of these ancient buildings.

Eric Bouvet

A Serbian fighter pauses near his howitzer between rounds, fully engaged in the fight to redress injustices inflicted on his people since they lost the Battle of Kosovo to the Turks in 1389. For him, it is nothing less than a fight for his nation's survival. "We can fight alone if we have to," as one Serbian soldier said. "We are not afraid to die."

Laurent van der Stockt

*T*he *Bridge on the Drina*, written by Nobel laureate Ivo Andric, a Bosnian Serb, is a lovely memoir of Bosnia. It narrates all the ingredients of the historical and cultural synthesis on the riverbank. In one chapter, the rabbi has a solid part to play; in others, it is the imam or priest who has the last word. But most of all, the hero is the *kapia*—the fine stonework that surmounts the keystone of the bridge and furnishes a meeting place for all the commingled cultures. When, at the book's end, the span of the bridge is blown into the Drina after centuries of connectedness, even those who have never seen the Balkans feel a sense of loss.

And so when I decided to walk from the Presidency Building in Sarajevo toward the river, I had my eye on a landmark: a beautiful and dignified building in the middle distance. Sarajevans still kept up the idea of the stroll in August of 1992 and tried to preserve the decencies of the coffee shop and the neighborly exchange on the corner. (It was, as you swiftly learned, considered the height of ill manners to inquire whether a person were Muslim, Jewish, Catholic, or Orthodox.) My walk took me along the edge of the Bascarsija, an area of town largely built in wood and famous for its quaint lanes, old houses, and tiny market stalls.

A group of friendly drinkers hailed me as I passed the door of a café, and as I stood there, chatting, my destination became a target. A vicious screech and explosion announced a mortar shell. Even the hardened locals drew back and hunched a bit. The mortar had hit, just on the angle of the edifice, and just where I would have been if I'd kept walking. And what's that handsome building? I asked. "It is the national library of Bosnia."

By then, I had been up in the hills and realized that the gunners and snipers could see exactly what they were doing. Who, however anxious to capture a city, would take deliberate aim at such a splendid building, knowing it housed the archive of a distinctive civilization? More was under attack, in Sarajevo, than the civilians. More was at stake. When, many months later, I finished *The Bridge on the Drina*, and my mind's eye saw that arch of civilization fall into the river, breaking the contact between ancient and mutually fertile peoples and cultures, I was momentarily back in Sarajevo again. And hoping never to be asked what I had done to stop the destruction of Bosnia. The men who desecrated the library may have had their own motives, but where exactly *was* everybody while this torture of a city and a civilization was going on?

Christopher Hitchens

After repeated shelling, the city's Central Library is rendered a tragic husk of its former magnificence. The national library once housed millions of volumes, some dating to medieval times; officials and residents spirited many of them to safety in underground bunkers during the early days of the siege.

Noel Quidu

The Lion Cemetery on Sarajevo's Kosevo Hill used to be a calm, lush place with chestnut trees that offered merciful shade in the heat of mid-summer. A graveyard for partisan fighters, the cemetery saw no new burials for 25 years. But in the first week of July 1992, hundreds of fresh graves scarred the ground, with the dead clearly divided by religion: temporary crosses for Croats and Serbs, plain boards for Muslims, and markers with a red star for declared atheists. Walking among the new graves one Sunday afternoon, I met Danis Tanovic, a strikingly handsome 23-year-old wearing black jeans and a leather jacket.

Tanovic was hunched over a video camera, filming the rows of graves and a family in one corner of the cemetery who had come to mourn. He was a film student before the war, now making a documentary on Sarajevo he called *Cultural Genocide*. Like everyone else in Sarajevo that first summer of the siege, Tanovic seemed stunned by what was happening, unable to comprehend how centuries of uneasy yet peaceful coexistence among different ethnic groups had dissolved within weeks into merciless slaughter. "It's like a bad dream," he told me. "I can't believe how people you used to go around with, chase girls with, are out there somewhere shooting at your family, shooting at your sister."

Tanovic spoke with simple eloquence of the terrible consequences of the war. As a Muslim, he was scornful of suggestions that Sarajevo could be partitioned. The city's population was so intermingled—Serbs and Croats sharing the same floors of apartment buildings, Muslims and Jews tending shops next door to one another—that such a plan was to him a fantasy. "Are they going to segregate every building?" he asked. "This is a Serbian building; this is Muslim; this is a Croatian coffee shop? It's madness."

Tanovic seemed like a voice of moderation and reason amid chaos, except for one disturbing sign. In a leather pouch on his belt he kept a hand grenade, its detonating pin carefully taped shut. "Believe me," he said just before we parted, "if they catch me, I'll explode this. I'll kill myself and take a few of them with me. I think I'll go there [he pointed toward heaven] if I do that." Given what has happened to Sarajevo since we met, it seems more likely that he used the grenade than that he finished his film.

Andrew Phillips, *Maclean's*

Young Sarajevans dance during a spontaneous party in the Hrasno quarter, dangerously near the Serbian front lines. As the new year dawned, Sarajevans faced death, malnutrition, and hopelessness, but the city's brewery still pumped out Sarajevsko Pivo beer as it had since 1864— now watered down to extend its scant supply.

Patrick Chauvel

As the siege enters its tenth month, Sarajevo's destiny remains as ambiguous as the sardonic sign for victory flashed by a Bosnian youth.

Antoine Gyori

A boy's face reflects the resignation that became a common Sarajevan response to the disintegration of their society—a destruction not only of lives and families, but also of the niceties of civilized life, such as the removal of rotting garbage from the city's streets.

Ron Haviv

It was a crisp winter's day outside the Serbian barracks. Rays of sun glistened on the dry winter's earth, and the hills around the city looked almost benign. Only the occasional sniper's shot broke the stillness. Deeply dug-in tanks, their barrels pointed at blocks of apartments a mile or so away, guarded the road.

Suddenly the superficial calm was broken by the arrival of two mud-spattered buses. They creaked into the barracks and stopped. Thirty battered, dirty men in torn clothing, each clutching a plastic bag, tumbled out, unsure of their welcome or their surroundings, unsure of what to do next.

Unbidden, the crowd moved inside to a room filled with long tables. And sat. And waited. For the past eight months these Serbs had been held in Sarajevo's main prison just a mile or two away. Now they were free, thanks to French mediation. Bogdan had once worked in a factory manufacturing radios. Alexander had been an office worker, Viktor a pensioner. None was under 60. Their gaunt eyes and wary glances dominated the taut atmosphere.

Bogdan's mistake had been to keep a hunting gun in his flat; he was accused of storing weapons when Muslims took over his neighborhood. Alexander had been picked up walking down the street. Viktor had been denounced by his next-door neighbor. After eight months in prison, Bogdan lost 66 pounds, surviving on a diet of tea in the morning and 12 grams of bread—about one half-slice—at night. Most of his time, he said, was spent outside a barracks held by the Muslims. Occasionally he would join a work gang cleaning the streets of Sarajevo; several times passersby stopped and beat him up.

The prisoners said they had been guarded by "thugs" imported from Sandzhak, a Muslim-dominated area in Serbia. One name, Kemal Dautovic, recurred in the endless stories of beating and torture. Viktor recalled 13 of his friends who had been beaten to death by the guards in nightly orgies of violence. In a matter-of-fact voice, Alexander recalled being hung from a hook in his cell for 24 hours.

To one side of the room, a daughter gazed unblinkingly at her father. Silent and bowed, he said nothing. She persisted with her questions. Eventually he mumbled something. She clutched his arm. "It's over, it's over," she reassured the old man. His staring, vacant eyes told another story.

Robin Knight, *U.S. News & World Report*

A mother and her daughter gaze at family members—perhaps for the last time—moments before they are evacuated from the city by bus. Thousands of families were fragmented during the siege: men and older Sarajevans stayed behind, while women and children, when they could escape the city, left for refugee centers, most commonly in Croatia, Germany, and Hungary.

Luc Delahaye

While one boy uses his sled to collect scraps of wood, others brave an apparent lull in the shelling to play in the deserted streets. Fortunately the winter of 1992–93 was relatively mild, and dire predictions of up to 400,000 weather-related deaths throughout Bosnia did not materialize.

Left: Peter Northall
Right: Patrick Durand

On Christmas Eve, 1992, a man gathers firewood, hacking at a tree stump in a cemetery. Soldiers and officials were given passes to chop down the city's beloved trees, leaving other citizens no choice but to forage for firewood among their leftover stumps. Birds, suddenly bereft of a place to land or nest, abandoned the city.

Jon Jones

Following pages: As 1992 ends, Muslim mourners brave sniper fire and bitter cold to entomb their dead. Funerals became increasingly brief ceremonies attended by few women.

Thomas Kern

I was awakened by the angry wailing of a boy in the courtyard below my eighth-floor window. It seemed at first to be just the protest of a child upset in play, but he did not let up, and his voice grew steadily more desperate.

Looking down, I saw the boy standing in a shallow pit, next to a partially dug-up tree stump. A man was sitting on the stump, as if to claim it, but the boy also wanted it, and he was in a tearful fury. I had watched people from the neighborhood taking turns at the stump for three days, hacking off bits of wood to be burned in their kitchen stoves. The boy's father must have sent him to the stump early this morning with instructions to hold it, because the boy stood his ground as though the survival of his whole family were at stake. But the man sitting on the stump refused to move. A passerby stopped in response to the boy's anguished cries. Only then did the man on the stump say anything. He waved his hand dismissively at the boy and, pointing to the stump, said something loudly to the passerby, who moved on then without intervening.

There was little to quarrel over. The main portion of the stump was already chopped off; this was a fight over what was underground. Several hours of hacking, however, could still yield enough wood chips to fill a large plastic bag. Three other stumps nearby had already been dug up and the holes in the earth refilled. The contested stump was the last bit of wood left in the ground.

These had been big trees. This barren lot behind my building must have been a shaded and leafy garden before the people of the neighborhood had taken to it with their axes and saws. Wood was now the only fuel left in Sarajevo. The only bread to be had was that baked at home over a wood fire. What water could be collected was contaminated and needed to be boiled. And now the search for chips and twigs left a neatly dressed man and a boy in sneakers facing each other meanly over a hole in the ground.

The boy's unrelenting whine soon attracted a small crowd. A discussion ensued, and somehow the dispute was resolved. By afternoon the last of the stump had been dug up and taken away. Two men were by then digging off to the side of the pit, having unearthed a lateral root of the tree, at least six inches thick.

Tom Gjelten, National Public Radio

As winter grips the city, hungry dogs roam Sarajevo's streets in the numbing cold; as their hunger worsened, former pets became dangerous, often biting at children and older Sarajevans. *At right:* Without heat or water at home, a woman washes her family's clothes in the freezing Miljacka River.

Left: Andrew Reid
Right: Jon Jones

Following pages: The day before Christmas, 1992, a man pushes his water containers home past the mounds of refuse piled on every corner. Thousands of middle-class Sarajevans became solitary scavengers, fending for themselves after their families fled or were killed.

Jon Jones

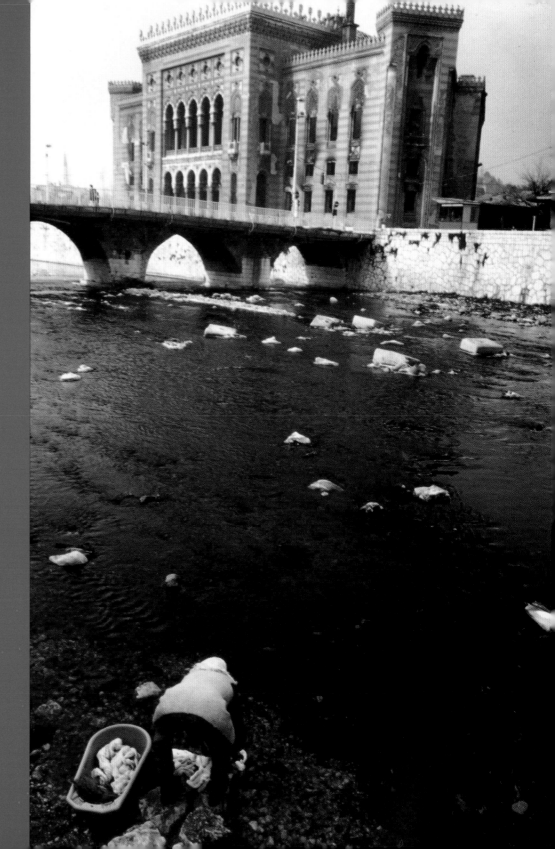

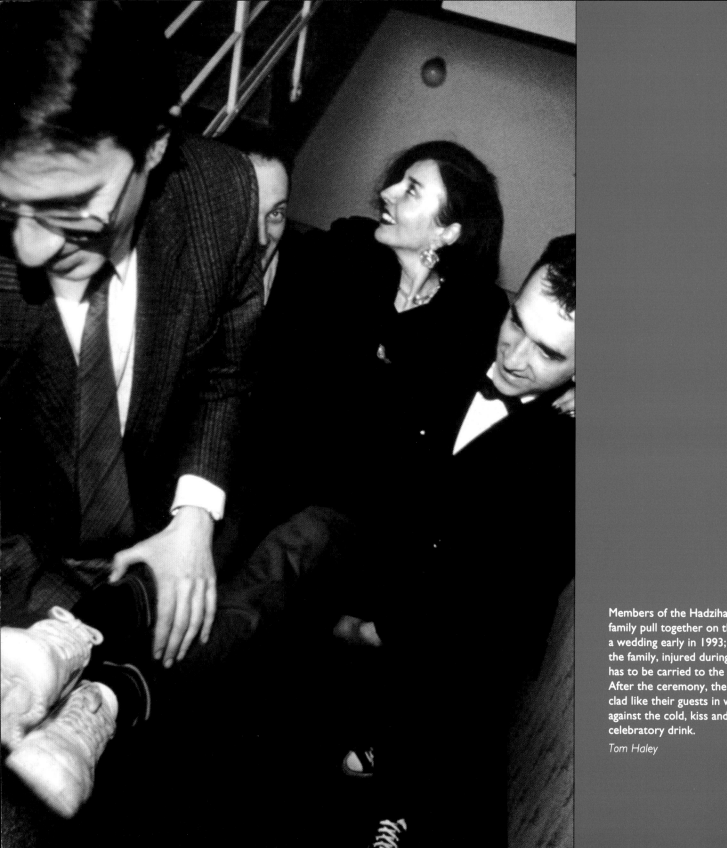

Members of the Hadzihal Ilovic
family pull together on their way to
a wedding early in 1993; a friend of
the family, injured during the siege,
has to be carried to the gathering.
After the ceremony, the newlyweds,
clad like their guests in winter coats
against the cold, kiss and enjoy a
celebratory drink.

Tom Haley

Vedad Hamdic's fever wouldn't go down. No one could help the 10-month-old infant in the devastated and isolated Sarajevo suburb of Sokolovic Kolonija, which had no doctors and a single overworked nurse. His father, Zijo, a policeman, had the local authorities lodge a desperate plea with the United Nations Protection Force: could they safely take his baby through the Serbian noose around Sarajevo and in to Kosevo Hospital, only six miles away?

They could not, for UNPROFOR had by then allowed a cruel parity to govern its actions. Unless UN authorities could balance that transport with a similar one for a Serbian patient, the Serbs would refuse passage; unwilling to use force, UNPROFOR acquiesced to the power of those who would. For five days, while Vedad's condition worsened, Zijo and his wife, Zlatka, held a gruesome vigil for word of a sickened Serb. Finally they decided they would have to risk their own lives to save their baby.

On three consecutive nights, Zijo and Zlatka lay for hours with Vedad in a trench laced with barbed wire along the Sarajevo airport, waiting for a moment to run through Serbian snipers along the runway and get into the city. Three times they were turned back by the UN soldiers who discouraged such crossings. One soldier met the parents' pleas for mercy by saying that Vedad wasn't sick, just sleeping. On the fourth night they made the dash, but by the time they reached Kosevo Hospital, it was too late. Vedad died the next day of encephalitis, a disease that responds well to timely treatment. Dr. Bisera Vranic, the specialist who treated Vedad, voiced the anger that has grown with every passing month in the besieged city: "All guilt is on UNPROFOR for the death of this child."

Humanitarian aid is a mockery when offered only in the thrall of the aggressor. Little wonder that Vedad's relatives and thousands of other Bosnians have gradually come to consider it worse than nothing at all. "It would be better if UNPROFOR just left," said the baby's aunt Melca. "The little food aid we get doesn't enter the balance. They can't even protect little children." On the day Vedad was buried in a crowded Sarajevo cemetery, his parents heard about the heinous shelling of a soccer game in Dobrinja, not far from where they had left their other child, four-year-old Edita, with relatives. "They said, 'We lost one child and don't want to lose the other one,' then left to cross the runway again," said Melca, quietly weeping. "I don't even know if they made it." If they did, they were doomed—like Sarajevo itself—to face their loss alone.

James Graff, *Time*

Three boys stand among Serbian and Muslim graves, dug between suburban apartment buildings once it became too dangerous to carry bodies into town to a cemetery.

Zeljko Maganjic

One particularly hot day, we had just come out of the French commiss-ary at the Sarajevo airport with three cartons of chocolate-coated, vanilla ice cream cones. As we waited for our colleagues to bring the armored car around, this treasure sat on the macadam and started to dribble through its seams. A gaggle of boys circled us, begging for a cone. They were 10- to 12-year-olds, on bikes with raised handlebars and raked frames, the kind that do wheelies so well. They wore tee-shirts and shorts, and high-top sneakers; a couple of them were carrying those cobalt-blue and gray-green nylon rucksacks so popular now for book bags. These kids weren't students but runners; at night they dashed from the Muslim lines east of the airport to the Muslim "free territory" west of the airport, across the runways, braving Serbian snipers with infrared scopes who have the drop on them for at least 200 yards. They return with the essentials of frontline life: cigarettes and bullets. The Muslims send boys to do this job, not because Serbian snipers wouldn't shoot children, but because kids make smaller targets.

The boys' leader was Mustafa, 11 years old, who went beyond begging to offer dollars and even deutsche marks for something they hadn't had in a year. We told him we couldn't take his money. In final desperation, he took out a flip-top box of Marlboros. "You're all too young to smoke," someone said. Mustafa laughed. "Not too young to get shot at." In some silly way, it seemed a double philanthropy if we both gave the boys ice cream and took away their smokes, so we drove a hard bargain of one pack per cone. They ate them very slowly, appreciatively, as if such luck might never come again. It was about the happiest we'd ever seen a bunch of kids in Sarajevo. One of the boys handed over an extra box of Marlboros, for nothing. "I'm quitting," he said.

The next day we were driving across the airport, but in daylight and with permission, in our "hard" armored car. On the runway was what could have been one of those boys' blue-and-green rucksacks, smeared across the tarmac in a mess of blood and grime, as if some gargantuan foot had descended suddenly and squashed what ran there. We didn't dare stop.

Rod Nordland, *Newsweek*

Two members of a gang of orphaned teenagers warm themselves near an intersection. As casualties mounted and refugees from outlying towns streamed into the city, thousands of children became orphaned or forgotten.

Luc Delahaye

While the mass of Sarajevans struggle against lives of quiet desperation, these youngsters find easy companionship in street gangs. They loot relief agency trucks and sell the goods on the black market, often to buy pastries and glue to sniff.

Luc Delahaye

Sarajevans buy cigarettes—a commodity that became as rare as food—from the back of a truck.

Filip Horvat

Orphans chase a humanitarian relief truck across an intersection. If they catch it, they will hang on to the tailgate, peer under the canvas cover, and use pocketknives to slice open the aid boxes, stuffing tinned beef, cheese, oil, or sugar into their pockets.

Luc Delahaye

Following pages: Young boys play war with toy guns and a discarded rocket launcher in February 1993. Some launchers fired only one round and were then thrown away.

Patrick Chauvel

Sarajevans hurriedly cross a narrow girder, all that is left of Shepherd's Bridge, on their way to queue for a daily ration of water. Like other water routes, the bridge was often targeted by Serbian snipers after the city's main pumping station was destroyed.

Luc Delahaye

A man makes his way home through rubble-strewn streets with precious loaves of bread. Early in the siege, the number of working bakeries dwindled as bombing continued and relief shipments became sporadic; later, even the city's main bakery would often run out of fuel and close for days at a time. The average Sarajevan lost 20 to 30 pounds during the siege.

Steve Connors

In the suburb of Dobrinja, a woman runs a sniper's gauntlet between a welcome corridor of sandbags on her way to get water. Sarajevans soon learned to hide for hours near public spigots, waiting for snipers to fall asleep or move their positions.

Luc Delahaye

Muris Osmanagic, in his mid-60s, was a mining engineer and university professor in the former Yugoslavia. Now he and his wife, Tonka, live in a second-floor apartment near the oldest part of Sarajevo, relying on humanitarian aid for their daily subsistence. Their three sons have left for the United States. Each day, Muris dresses in a business suit and tie and walks three kilometers to bring back water for him and his wife to use that day. Muris is Muslim, Tonka Croatian. Muris talked to Michael Tharp one day during his walk.

For the water! For us it is golden. It is life. I am going through the city now to fill up my water jugs, and will meet many of my friends along the way. I am a scientist and will wear my daily professional clothes—not farmers' clothes.

We have to use the same water for cooking, washing and laundry, and the toilet. For two months we had no water after the Chetniks destroyed the city's main pump. My wife and I together need 20 liters of water a day.

This is the old town where craftsmen used to make copper products, and that is the Central Library, now completely destroyed. These terrorists particularly like to destroy culture.

[He raises an open-fingered right hand, akin to showing a count of five, in greeting to a white-haired man.] That is the traditional Bosnian greeting—open hand and heart. Like the native Indians in America. That is what the UN wants to do, put us on reservations like Indians. But never, never, never.

[After filling the jugs at the public spigots, he ties them with a belt over his shoulder and starts home.]

I look forward to the time when Serbs, Croats, and Muslims will live together again on a personal basis, when people will look at each other as individuals, as men and women again.

This is my break point. [He stops in a small plaza in front of a shell-pocked building and switches the belt and jugs to his other shoulder.] On May 27, the Chetniks had their artillery coordinates set on the people in line right here for bread. Twenty-two were killed, 90 wounded.

If barbarism wins in the Balkans, it will win in the former Soviet Union, in Europe. The United States will remain isolated. It is not a problem of money, of who can pay for the biggest guns. It is a problem of life, of the whole civilization, of what is decent and right.

Up the hill and we are home.

Muris Osmanagic, as told to Michael Tharp,
U.S. News & World Report

Sarajevans fill their homemade grenades with gunpowder and their flasks with water.

Left: Tom Haley
Right: Luc Delahaye

On one of the city's many front lines, a Bosnian soldier shades his rifle scope while searching for targets. Some of the frontline positions, such as a joint Muslim-Croatian strongpoint near the ravaged Parliament Building, were no more than the gutted ruins of buildings.

Antoine Gyori

Bosnian army mechanics take a cigarette break. By February 1993, supplies of tobacco had become so rare that lines of Sarajevans, three and four abreast, stretched for blocks near rationing points, and armed soldiers occasionally broke up fights among those waiting for cigarettes. That winter, a carton went for DM50 (about $33) on the black market; the price would soon jump to DM80, or $50.

Ron Haviv

Bosnian Muslim women on patrol as frontline soldiers in March 1993 defend their borough of Sarajevo, Pofalici, in the hills above the city. Most women as well as men were expected to serve the war effort: only children, women over 55, and men over 60 were exempt from military or other wartime service. Among the Sarajevan women who served, fully 1 in 10 volunteered for frontline duty.

Luigi Baldelli

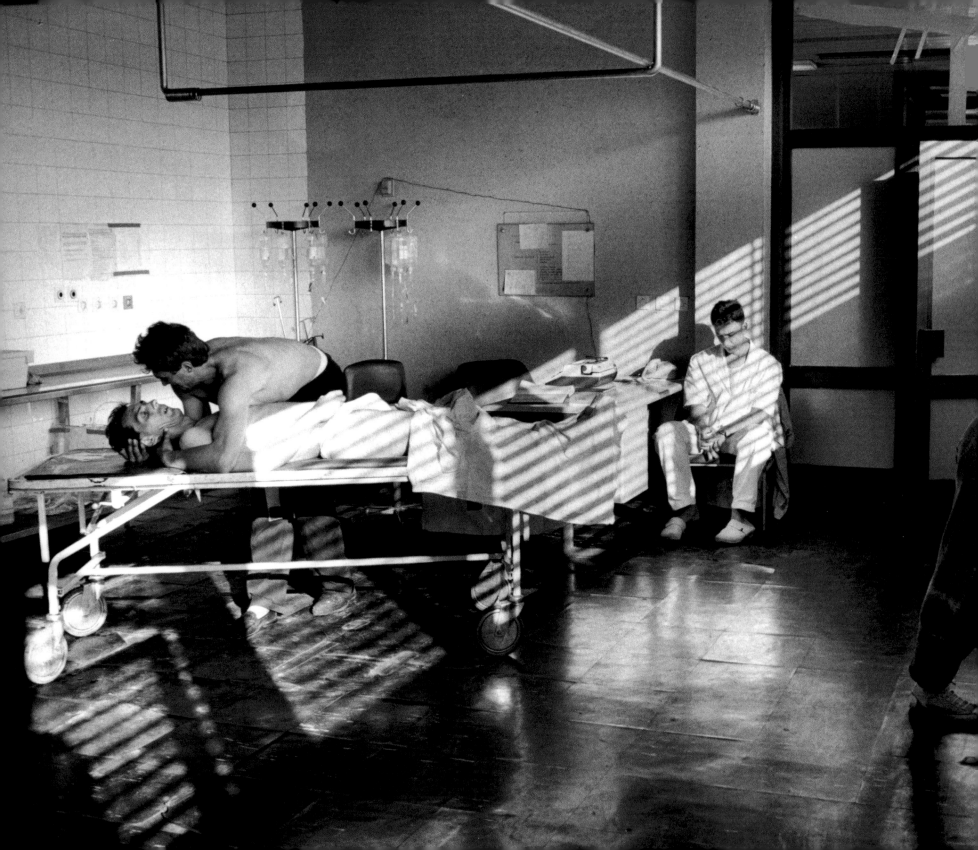

Despite the efforts of two doctors, Remzija Aljukic, a Muslim soldier shot by a sniper in July 1993, dies on the operating table. Two of his brothers—also soldiers—attend his last moments, one cradling the dead man, the other overcome by his grief at the window of Kosevo Hospital.

Luc Delahaye

Following pages: **A panoramic view of Sarajevo eastward from the Parliament Building.**

Gary Knight

D r. Sanja Besarovic is struggling to save a man who's been shot by a sniper. This time she doesn't make it, and the dead man's brother is crying as he leaps at the doctor and tries to hit her. She thinks maybe it's because she's a Serb and the dead man and his family are Muslims. This is Sarajevo.

But Doctor Sanja, as she is called here, tells me this kind of reaction is rare, that most of her Muslim patients and their families adore her. They walk for miles to come back and visit her, to bring her gifts, to thank her, for she has chosen to stay in Sarajevo under siege, patching up the broken and battered bodies that are carried into her operating theater, victims of her compatriots' firing from the hills above. Those Serbs tell me that any of their own who have stayed in Sarajevo are "bad Serbs." They are wrong.

Doctor Sanja has volunteered to work 48-hour shifts instead of the usual 24. Each week, she is allowed one day off, when she looks after her mother, collects water, cuts wood, and looks for food. And then she's back again, cutting and stitching by candlelight . . . with torches . . . with a miner's lamp wrapped around her head. There is rarely any electricity, even at the hospital, and not enough drugs, anesthetics, or water. But there are so many wounded: on a bad day 200 people can be rushed to the emergency room. Doctor Sanja and her colleagues once performed 46 operations in one shift; she simply never gives up. Once a senior surgeon told her to amputate an eight-year-old child's leg, a girl who had been hit by shrapnel. Doctor Sanja refused, and instead worked on the little girl, who was still lying on her stretcher since the operating tables were all occupied. Doctor Sanja saved the leg, and smiled as she described how the child can walk and even run.

When I last spoke to her, Doctor Sanja had not succumbed to the forces that are tearing Sarajevo's people apart. "I am proud I am a Serb," she said. "I am proud I stayed and proud of my Muslim and Croatian friends. Nothing has changed between us. I think as a doctor; I am not on any side. I don't look at a patient and wonder who he is, just is he alive and can I save him."

Christiane Amanpour, CNN

113

EPILOGUE

Throughout most of the siege, the journalists were perhaps the only dependable allies the Sarajevans had; their words and photographs kept the siege alive—to the extent that it could be kept alive—in the minds of Western Europeans and North Americans. The Bosnian government, which had bet everything on foreign intervention, understood the influence of the foreign press corps early on. It also understood that, deprived of any means of defending itself by a UN-imposed arms embargo that only prevented the government side from resupplying itself, foreign sympathy was practically the only lever at its disposal. The journalists' accounts were the best way of mobilizing this sympathy, and there were times when the Bosnian authorities seemed actually to welcome the photo opportunity that some particular atrocity provided them.

And why shouldn't they have? The world had recognized Bosnia-Herzegovina and then abandoned it to the Serbian onslaught. And as the fighting continued, and the prospect of a Bosnian defeat hardened into a certainty, the European Community, the permanent members of the UN Security Council, and the United Nations Secretariat decided that even recognition of the Sarajevo government had been an error. Soon, foreign politicians and the negotiators charged by the UN and the EC with finding a solution to the conflict "demoted" the Bosnians and began to speak of the Muslim, Serbian, and Croatian sides, just as, 60 years earlier, their predecessors in the League of Nations had spoken, not of the Spanish Republic and its rebel enemies, but of "Republican" and "Nationalist" sides. The only weapon the Sarajevans had in ample supply was their own suffering. And if they sometimes waited to remove a body until the foreign journalists had arrived, or sometimes seemed almost masochistic in their refusal to negotiate arrangements that might have secured a little more electricity or gas for Sarajevo, this did not mean, as UN officials in Zagreb sometimes liked to contend, that they were somehow the authors of their own suffering.

Where the Bosnians made their mistake was in believing that, if somehow people in the outside world could take in what was happening to Sarajevo, their long-awaited foreign intervention would

A car's windshield reflects a year of sound and fury in Sarajevo. By then, the Serbs held 70% of Bosnia-Herzegovina, the Bosnian government estimated 137,000 dead on all sides throughout Bosnia, and the city's prewar population of 526,000 had shrunk to 380,000.

Gary Knight

finally come. From the spring of 1992 to the midsummer of 1993—when Sarajevans, perpetual optimists though they improbably were, finally and definitively lost hope in the deus ex machina of American airstrikes and in the misnamed United Nations Protection Force—every journalist who spent time in Sarajevo heard time and time again the injunction "Tell the world what is going on in Sarajevo."

They—we—tried. They—we—failed. Perhaps the foreign press corps in the Holiday Inn had, as a BBC reporter at the UN in New York once put it to me offensively, simply gone too native. Sitting in a room in the Holiday Inn late at night, drinking the latest bottle of malt some recent arrival had brought in from Split or Ancona, after a day spent on the front line, or in the casualty ward of the French hospital, or among the people scrambling along denuded hillsides (Sarajevo used to be known for its parks), it seemed incredible to us that the world could be indifferent to what was going on in Bosnia, or worse, could imagine that what was going on was just some ancient ethnic conflict—just another Balkan war where no side was really all that much better than any other. Surely one more picture, or one more story, or one more correspondent's "stand-up" taped in front of a shelled building would bring people around, would force them to stop shrugging their shoulders or blaming their victims. And so the stories were satellite-faxed to New York, Paris, London, and Washington; the photos carried out to the world's busiest agencies; and the television segments transmitted, sometimes live, to CNN and ITN and Antenne 2. Moreover, the editors back home gave these reports and images an enormous amount of play. In the future, no one will be able to say, as Germans legitimately said during the Second World War, that they did not know what was going on in Bosnia. The press may ultimately have failed, but it did its job. No slaughter was more scrupulously and ably covered.

In truth, the international press corps has sympathized with Sarajevo to a degree that is altogether out of character for this group of professional skeptics. In a world where the diplomats and politicians who could have done something to save Bosnia have seemed determined to watch as it is destroyed, as the third great genocide of a European minority is carried out, journalists found that they believed in "Western values" even as the Western political elite continued to betray them. Sarajevo has seemed unique to all but the most corrupt members of the press who have spent any time there. Men and women who have seen countless wars and thought themselves inured to suffering, and who came to Bosnia thinking that it was just one more assignment, have ended caring about what has happened there in decidedly unprofessional ways. Not only has the Bosnian war cost more foreign journalists their lives than any conflict since World War II, but it has also engaged them in ways that they have not been engaged since the forties. John Burns is only the most celebrated of a large number of reporters and photojournalists who have insisted on returning to Sarajevo again and again, even when prudential careerism would have dictated moving on to other, fresher venues.

Now, of course, though the journalists return, the sad truth is that they are less welcome. Sarajevans have finally understood that there will be no intervention, and these days, even one's friends in Sarajevo are likely to look askance when one arrives in town fresh from an outside world that now seems as mythical as heaven. Instead of bringing photojournalists to the scene of the latest breadline massacre or schoolroom massacre or funeral sniping, many Sarajevans speak bitterly of foreign photographers' installing themselves at dangerous street corners waiting for someone to get shot. "Angels of death," they are called. And at the hospitals where, when nothing else is going on, the print reporters tend to congregate, doctors speak of charging admission. The change of mood is understandable. Not only are Sarajevans in a mood to shoot the messengers who failed them, however hard those messengers may have tried; the fact that the handwriting is on the wall and that, at present anyway, there is little hope of any decent outcome in Bosnia further devalues the journalists' presence in the city. Now they are interlopers, unwanted voyeurs of the Bosnian death agony. And those reporters who still remain in Sarajevo do not entirely disagree. They are ashamed of their countries, ashamed of their failure to move their viewers and readers, and though more mutedly, ashamed of their profession.

But most of all, the photojournalists and reporters—the best ones anyway—will never recover from the experience of Sarajevo. A deep commitment gave their work its edge, even as it broke their hearts. As well it should have. For as it turns out, all the pieties about the Holocaust, the declarations of "never again," meant nothing. Knowledge is not power, after all. The images and descriptions of the Bosnian war have touched millions and, as the war recedes, will remain, like unexploded landmines, ready to trigger the shame that those who have watched and done nothing will perhaps someday feel. They are acts of witness, and need no further justification. But they have not saved Bosnia or even Sarajevo. The disgrace is complete.

David Rieff

Beneath a surviving rim in the city's financial district, two boys play in a city where some neighborhoods resembled London in 1940 and Berlin in 1945. Only weeks into the siege, Ratko Mladic, a Serbian general, had told his troops in the hills: "Burn it all."

Tom Stoddart

THE PHOTOGRAPHERS

Epicenter Communications made every attempt to retrieve background information for photographers **Zeljko Maganjic** and **Truman Moore**; we regret the omission of their biographical notes.

Bill Bachman
Widely known for his photography and writing on skiing, Bachman has worked as a freelance photographer and journalist since 1981. His images have appeared in a wide variety of publications, including *Australian Geographic, This Australia,* and *Discovery.* Bachman's pictorial diary of his travels in Australia's outback, *Off the Road Again,* was published in 1989, and his most recent work, *Local Colour,* was published by Odyssey Productions in September 1993.

Luigi Baldelli
Rome-based photojournalist Luigi Baldelli began his career in 1983, covering Italian national news. He began working with the Contrasto photo agency in 1987 and, since then, has covered the Romanian Revolution, the coup in Pakistan, and the Gulf War and ensuing Kurdish refugee crisis. Baldelli has covered the war in the former Yugoslavia since its beginning, based in Zadar, Croatia, and Sarajevo.

Eric Bouvet
Since joining Saga Images in 1992, French photojournalist Eric Bouvet's work has appeared in publications internationally, including *Time, Life, Der Spiegel, The Sunday Times Magazine* of London, and *Paris Match.* Since 1985, he has traveled widely on assignment, covering events in Northern Ireland, Libya, Afghanistan, South Africa, the Persian Gulf, and lately the former Yugoslavia; his work has earned him several World Press Photo awards.

David Brauchli
From his base in Prague, David Brauchli has covered Africa and Europe for the Associated Press since April 1992. Previously he spent several years working in Hong Kong, Prague, and London for Reuters, and in Moscow for Agence France Presse. In May 1992, he spent three weeks in Sarajevo, where he was wounded by a shell. He is currently working in South Africa, covering the elections for the AP. Brauchli is represented by the Sygma photo agency.

Patrick Chauvel
Chauvel has worked as a photojournalist since the Middle East's Six-Day War in 1967, producing stories for *France-Soir* magazine, Sipa Press, and since 1975, the Sygma photo agency. He has covered many war zones, including Vietnam, Northern Ireland, Angola, Iran, and Haiti, sometimes spending several months at a time with an army. Chauvel has published stories in various international magazines, and in 1989, he photographed the American invasion of Panama for *Newsweek.*

Steve Connors
Having begun photography as a hobby while serving in the British army, Connors began his career documenting industrial and urban decay in his hometown of Sheffield, England. In 1984, he went to work as a photojournalist in London, following his efforts there with a 1989 trip to Prague to cover the student-led uprisings. Since 1991, when he joined the Select photo agency, he has produced a body of work on the war in the former Yugoslavia, much of it published in magazines internationally.

Jerry Cooke
Born and educated in Europe, Cooke began his photographic career in 1943. His work has been published in magazines worldwide and is represented in several museum collections. Cooke served as a picture editor at *Sports Illustrated* and as president and a board member of the American Society of Magazine Photographers. He lives currently in East Hampton, New York.

Luc Delahaye
Since joining Sipa Press in 1985, Delahaye has covered major world conflicts, including the war in Lebanon, the Romanian Revolution and the fall of Ceaucescu, and the Gulf War. When Yugoslavia began to split, Delahaye had already decided to cover the war until its end. His images from Bosnia have earned him the Overseas Press Club 1993 Robert Capa Gold Medal and a 1993 first prize from the World Press Photo Foundation.

Corinne Dufka
Dufka first discovered an interest in photojournalism while working as a social worker in El Salvador. She began freelancing for international agencies and American newspapers, as well as human rights organizations like Amnesty International and Americas Watch. In 1989, she began working for Reuters, covering not only the civil war in El Salvador, but also regional events from Mexico to Panama. In early 1992, she was assigned to Bosnia, where she has covered the plight of Sarajevans under siege since June of that year.

Patrick Durand
Durand has been a photojournalist for almost 20 years. Following five years of freelancing and a stint with the French magazine *VSD,* he lived in the United States from 1980 to 1985, working as a foreign correspondent for *Paris Match* and *Le Figaro.* Since then, he has covered political unrest and conflicts in South Africa, Afghanistan, China, Romania, and the former Yugoslavia. He joined Sygma in 1986.

Frank Fournier
Fournier began his career as a photojournalist in 1972, following several years of medical training. Since then, he has produced award-winning images of the effects of Colombia's Nevada del Ruiz volcano eruption, infant AIDS patients in Romania, and the medical aid organization Médecins sans Frontières. His work has earned him several World Press Photo awards and appeared in publications including *National Geographic, Time,* and *The New York Times Magazine.* He is represented by Contact Press Images.

Gianni Berengo Gardin
Gardin began his career in 1954 working for *Il Mondo,* then a leading Italian weekly magazine, and went on to publish his work in *Epoca* and publications of the De Agostini Geographic Institute. He has produced many books of photographs, and his images are on display at the Museum of Modern Art in New York, the Bibliothèque Nationale in Paris, and Peking's National Gallery of Art. He has lived in Milan since 1965.

Antoine Gyori
Gyori began his career in 1985 with a series of features on South America that was published in French and Brazilian newspapers. He went on to work for *France-Soir* and *Le Figaro* and, in April 1990, joined Sygma. Gyori has covered the rise of Islamic fundamentalism in Algeria and has reported on the former Yugoslavia since the start of the war in Bosnia. He was injured in Sarajevo in early 1993.

Patrice Habans
Habans has worked as a photographer since 1955, spending 17 years with *Paris Match* and going on to become assistant managing editor at the magazine. In 1979, he joined the staff of the Swiss magazine *Illustré,* leaving after a year to work as the official photographer of the Moscow Olympiad. He has been affiliated with Sygma since 1980.

Tom Haley
Sipa photojournalist Tom Haley has covered political conflicts in the Philippines, South Korea, and Panama. His work also includes coverage of the industrial disaster in Bhopal, India, the fall of the Berlin Wall, and the Gulf War. Since fighting began in the former Yugoslavia, Haley has made several trips there, recently producing an essay on a Sarajevo family. He and his family currently live in Paris.

Ron Haviv

Award-winning photojournalist Ron Haviv regularly publishes his work in *Time, Newsweek, Paris Match,* and *Stern.* Since becoming affiliated with the Saba Press photo agency in 1989, he has covered the invasion of Panama, the fall of the Berlin Wall, the release of Nelson Mandela, the Gulf War, and the Bosnian war. Haviv is the recipient of several World Press Photo awards, the Leica Medal of Excellence, and an Overseas Press Club award.

Michael Hayman

Hayman began his career as a photojournalist while he was a student, going on to work for *The Detroit Free Press, The Miami Herald, National Geographic,* and *The Flint Journal.* Since 1983, he has worked for *The Louisville Courier-Journal,* sharing the newspaper's Pulitzer Prize for a story on events following a tragic drunk driving accident.

Filip Horvat

Horvat has worked as a photojournalist for 15 years and has been represented by Saba Press since 1989. He has traveled widely, covering the Ethiopian drought of 1984, the fall of the Berlin Wall, the Iran/Iraq War, the Gulf War, and recently the civil strife in the Balkans. Born in Vinkovci in the former Yugoslavia, Horvat now lives in Zagreb, Croatia.

Anto Jelavic

Jelavic was born in Metkovic, Croatia, but has spent many years in Sarajevo as a student and later as a freelance photographer. His work appeared in various newspapers in Zagreb and Belgrade before he joined the Zagreb daily *Vecernji* in 1971. He received an award from the Bosnian press association in 1978 and went on to cover the 1984 Olympic Games.

Jon Jones

Born in Kampala, Uganda, Jones began his career as a photojournalist in Britain, working for a national news agency in England and spending three years as a photographer for the London *Independent.* He joined Sygma in 1991 and continues to cover events for the agency in the former Yugoslavia, Armenia, South Africa, and Somalia. In 1991, he won the Nikon News Photographer of the Year award and was a runner-up for British Telecom's Feature Photographer of the Year award.

Thomas Kern

Since beginning his career in 1987, Kern has covered stories in Northern Ireland, France, Iraq, and the former Yugoslavia. Exhibitions of his work have appeared in Zurich, Cairo, and Cologne, and his images have been published regularly in *Das Magazin* and *Liberation.* In 1993, he covered the plight of Bosnian refugees fleeing to Switzerland, and spent six months in Sarajevo for *du* magazine, and in other areas of Bosnia reporting on the effects of the war.

Gary Knight

Knight has worked as a professional photographer for seven years, spending most of that time in Southeast Asia. He has covered the riots in Bangkok, the wars in Burma and Kashmir, and the political, military, and social implications of the ongoing conflict in Cambodia. In May 1992, Knight joined Saba Press Photos; he has worked in Sarajevo and central Bosnia since January 1993.

James Mason

Mason began his career working as a stringer for the Associated Press. He became a freelancer in 1980, producing his first extensive photographic story on the eruption of Mount St. Helens that year. Educated in the former Yugoslavia, Mason has been based in Vitez, Bosnia, since 1992, working as a translator for the Associated Press, and covering events in the region for the Black Star photo agency.

Christopher Morris

Award-winning photojournalist Christopher Morris has covered political situations overseas for a decade, traveling to Europe, the Philippines, Central and South America, Africa, the former Soviet Union, and the Middle East. He has won awards for his coverage of the U.S. invasion of Panama, Liberia's civil war, and the riots in London over the notorious poll tax. In 1992, he was awarded the Robert Capa Gold Medal from the Overseas Press Club for his work in the former Yugoslavia.

Peter Northall

British photojournalist Peter Northall has been affiliated with the Black Star photo agency since 1991. In the two years since he began working on assignment for the agency, he has traveled in the former Yugoslavia, covering the conflict and its effects in that region.

Noel Quidu

French-born photojournalist Quidu has been affiliated with the Gamma photo agency for six years. He has covered stories in Lebanon, Jordan, and Afghanistan and in Iraq and Kuwait during the Gulf War. During the past two years, he has traveled in Bosnia and Croatia, chronicling the effect of the war in the Balkans.

Andrew Reid

Reid is a New Zealand–born photojournalist who has worked in North Africa and Germany. Since the outbreak of war in Croatia in mid-1991, he has covered the war in the former Yugoslavia almost exclusively. His images have appeared in publications internationally, including *Time, Newsweek, Paris Match, Stern,* and *Der Spiegel;* he is affiliated with the Gamma Liaison photo agency.

Tom Stoddart

Since joining Katz Pictures in 1989, Stoddart has covered the fall of the Berlin Wall, the Romanian Revolution, the Gulf War, and the Kurds in northern Iraq. His work has been published internationally since 1978, and he has twice received the U.K. Nikon Photographer of the Year award. In the summer of 1992, he traveled to Sarajevo on assignment for *The Sunday Times* of London and was wounded there in fighting near the Bosnian Parliament Building.

Laurent van der Stockt

Van der Stockt has spent the past several years covering political conflicts for Gamma. His work documents the Romanian Revolution, fighting in Israel, the Gulf War in Iraq, and oil fires in Kuwait. In September 1991, he was wounded in Vukovar, Croatia, but returned to work the following year, covering Bosnia again in 1993.

Art Zamur

Award-winning photojournalist Art Zamur has published his work in magazines internationally, including *Stern, Geo, Paris Match, Time,* and *Life.* He has also produced two books of his images—*Gypsies of the World,* which was published in six countries, and *Medjugorje,* published in the former Yugoslavia. Born in Nis, Serbia, he is now based in Belgrade, where he is a contract photographer for the Gamma Liaison photo agency.

THE WRITERS

Michael Tharp   *Caption Writer*

Currently West Coast correspondent for *U.S. News & World Report*, Tharp has spent much of his career in Tokyo, working for *The Wall Street Journal*, *The New York Times*, and the *Far Eastern Economic Review*. He was also a U.S. Army correspondent in Vietnam from 1969 to 1970. In the past few years, Tharp has covered the Gulf War as a member of the U.S. Army Combat Pool, Operation Restore Hope in Somalia, and the war in the former Yugoslavia. He traveled to Bosnia in May 1993, visiting Sarajevo for several days.

Dean Toda   *Editorial Adviser*

Toda is currently assistant foreign editor for *The New York Times*. He has worked for the newspaper since 1985, and has been the *Times'* principal desk editor for Balkan news since 1991, working with Pulitzer Prize–winning reporter John Burns. Toda was a visiting journalism fellow at Duke University in the spring of 1992. He lives with his family in Garden City, New York.

Essayists

Christiane Amanpour

An award-winning CNN correspondent, Amanpour has reported from war zones for several years, covering the Gulf War, the break-up of the Soviet Union, and the civil war in Somalia, as well as the resulting refugee crises. Her reporting from the former Yugoslavia has earned her both the Livingston Award for Young Journalists and the bronze award from the Houston International Film Festival. Amanpour has been in Sarajevo almost continually since July 1992.

Karen Breslau

Breslau became a general editor at *Newsweek International* in January 1993 after serving as the magazine's Bonn/Berlin correspondent for three years. She has reported on the collapse of the Berlin Wall, the Romanian Revolution, and the reunification of Germany. In April 1993, Breslau and three other *Newsweek* correspondents received a citation for excellence from the Overseas Press Club for their coverage of the war in the former Yugoslavia. She covered the Balkan war from the summer of 1991 until the fall of 1992, visiting Sarajevo several times.

John F. Burns

British-born writer John F. Burns, correspondent for *The New York Times*, has been based in Sarajevo since March 1992; his coverage of the war in Bosnia earned him a 1993 Pulitzer Prize. He has worked for *The Times* since 1975, reporting from Africa, China, Canada, the Soviet Union, and the former Yugoslavia. In 1979, he shared the prestigious George Polk award for foreign correspondence with two other *Times* correspondents.

Janine di Giovanni

Di Giovanni began her career in journalism as a reporter for the Associated Press. She has reported from Latin America and the Middle East and now lives in Britain, where she is a staff writer with *The Sunday Times* of London and a frequent contributor to *The Spectator*. Her first book, *Against the Stranger: Lives in Occupied Territories*, was published in January 1993. Di Giovanni has covered the war in the Balkans since September 1992, spending most of her time in Sarajevo.

Zlata Filipovic

Twelve-year-old Filipovic is a resident of Sarajevo whose diary was smuggled out of the city to be published in the summer of 1992. She was inspired by Anne Frank's wartime journal to chronicle both her daily experiences and the gradual destruction of the city throughout its siege.

Tom Gjelten

Gjelten has reported for National Public Radio from Berlin since 1990, covering the reunification of Germany, the dissolution of the former Soviet Union, and the Gulf War. He has spent 15 weeks in Sarajevo since the beginning of the war, and his ongoing coverage has earned him both an Overseas Press Club award and a 1993 George Polk award. He is currently working on a book about Sarajevo, to be published by HarperCollins in 1994.

James Graff

Graff, Central Europe bureau chief for *Time*, has worked for the magazine since 1983 from bases in Munich, Bonn, and Ottawa. Since early 1991, he has covered post-Communist Europe, including the former Yugoslavia. In February 1993, Graff was 1 of 10 journalists to visit the Bosnian enclave of Gorazde, which had been isolated for 10 months. Now based in Vienna, Graff has visited Sarajevo several times since February 1992, most recently in June 1993.

Brian Hall

Hall is the author of *The Impossible Country: A Journey through the Last Days of Yugoslavia*, to be published in the spring of 1994, and *Stealing from a Deep Place: Travels in Southeastern Europe* (1988). His work has also appeared in *The New York Times Magazine*. Hall has twice been to Sarajevo, once in May 1990 and again in June 1991. He and his family live in Ithaca, New York.

Christopher Hitchens

British writer Christopher Hitchens is a regular contributor to *The Nation* and *Vanity Fair*. Previously he served as foreign editor of the *New Statesman* and was a foreign correspondent for the *Daily Express*. Hitchens' books include *Prepared for the Worst* (1989) and *For the Sake of Argument* (1993), and he is currently at work on a book about Kurdistan, to be published in 1994. Hitchens visited Sarajevo in August 1992 to report for the *London Review of Books*.

Gordana Knezevic

Knezevic was born in Belgrade but has spent most of her adult life in Sarajevo. She began her career reporting for the local television station and one of the city's weekly magazines. Since 1980, she has worked for the Sarajevo newspaper *Oslobodenje*, as a correspondent and then as editor of the paper's political section. Since the war began, she has worked with the editor-in-chief, taking over for him when he was injured while trying to avoid sniper fire.

Robin Knight

Knight, who joined *U.S. News & World Report's* London bureau in 1968, is now the magazine's senior European editor. He has headed *U.S. News'* bureaus in Moscow, Johannesburg, and Rome and went on to work in Washington before returning to London in 1985. Since then, he has covered European affairs, traveling to the former Yugoslavia several times during the past few years. Knight visited Sarajevo in January 1993.

Rod Nordland

Nordland, *Newsweek's* Balkans correspondent, has reported from around the world, including Somalia, Nicaragua, Iraq, Kuwait, the Soviet Union, China, and South Africa. A prize-winning journalist, he has received two George Polk awards for foreign correspondence and shared the Philadelphia *Inquirer's* 1978 Pulitzer Prize for domestic reporting. Nordland visited Sarajevo frequently in 1993.

Andrew Phillips

Phillips was the London bureau chief for *Maclean's* magazine from 1988 to 1993, covering Europe and the Middle East. Previously he worked as a reporter and editor for *Maclean's*, the Canadian Broadcasting Corporation, and the Montreal *Gazette*. Born in British Columbia, Phillips is now senior editor for national affairs at the *Maclean's* Toronto office. He visited Sarajevo in the summer of 1992, returning in the spring of 1993.

David Rieff

David Rieff is the author of several books, including *Going to Miami* (1987), *Los Angeles: Capital of the Third World* (1992), and *The Exile: Cuba in the Heart of Miami* (1993), each examining American cities whose streets have been transformed by the influx of recent immigrants. He writes for *The New Yorker* magazine and is a contributing editor for *Harper's* magazine.

ACKNOWLEDGMENTS

Epicenter Communications would like to thank the international community of writers, photographers, and photographic agencies, as well as the following friends and colleagues, whose support has made this project possible. We also thank the countless Muslim, Croatian, Serbian, and Jewish families who have helped research photographs for this project and who, due to political realities in Sarajevo, have asked that they not be named.

Sheppy Abramowitz
John Altberg
Kuniumi Asai
Milton Batalion
Joel Brand
David Burnett
Jonathan Cartwright
Ingrid Castro
David Cohen
Guy Cooper
Josef Csallos
Darik
Michael Dashe
Sashka T. Dawg
Sandro Diani
Eastman Kodak Company, Professional
    Imaging Division
Maureen Mahon Egen
Sandra Eisert
Stephen Engelberg
Carey English
David Friend
Gerald S. Goldberg
David and Dianne Graeme-Baker
Anne Hamilton
Maureen Hargan
Acey Harper
Ron Haviv
Mike Hedges
Angus Hines
Bennett Hinkley
Ray Homer
Filip Horvat
Jeff Katz
Laurence Kirshbaum
Gary Knight
Roberto Koch
Rebecca Kondos
Harvey-Jane Kowal
Charles Lane

Ali Lejlic
Edin Lemes
Jeanette Lerman
Maya Levi
Alyssa Levy
Neno and Marenka Males
Doug Menuez
Mel Minter
Ivan Misic
Phillip Moffitt
Michael Moritz
John Morrissey
William T. Naythons
Bernard Ohanian
Daniel Okrent
Amila and Jasko Orucevic
Oslobodenje staff
Muris and Tonka Osmanagic
Laura Pitter
Robert Rabkin, MD
Jonathan Randall
Hillary Raskin
Tom Rielly
Sian Roberts
Lionel Rosenblatt
Michael D. Ryan
Omar Sacirbey
Barbara Sadick
William Sarnoff
Tony Smith
Tom Stoddart
Chuck Sudetic
SuperMAC Technology
Rebecca Swanston
John Sweeney
Judith Thurman
Gordon W. Tucker
Fiona Turner
Beka Vuco
Miriam Winocour

PHOTOGRAPHY CREDITS

1 Ethnographisches Museum
2 Ethnographisches Museum
4 Anto Jelavic
6 Tom Stoddart / Katz/Saba
8 Truman Moore / Black Star
10 Map © 1992 The New York Times Company
12 Jerry Cooke / Photo Researchers
14 Patrice Habans / Sygma
15 Ethnographisches Museum
16 Michael Hayman / Black Star
17 Gianni Berengo Gardin / Contrasto/Saba
18 Bill Bachman / Photo Researchers
19 Anto Jelavic
20 James Mason / Black Star
22 Truman Moore / Black Star
24 Ron Haviv / Saba
25 Ron Haviv / Saba
26 Andrew Reid / Gamma Liaison
27 Peter Northall / Black Star
28 Peter Northall / Black Star
29 David Brauchli / Sygma
30 Steve Connors / Select
31 Andrew Reid / Gamma Liaison
32 Tom Stoddart / Katz/Saba
33 Tom Stoddart / Katz/Saba
34 Jon Jones / Sygma
35 Christopher Morris / Black Star
36 Christopher Morris / Black Star
38 Patrick Chauvel / Sygma
40 Tom Stoddart / Katz/Saba
41 Tom Stoddart / Katz/Saba
42 Christopher Morris / Black Star
43 Patrick Chauvel / Sygma
44 Peter Northall / Black Star
46 Andrew Reid / Gamma Liaison
48 Andrew Reid / Gamma Liaison
50 Antoine Gyori / Sygma
51 Christopher Morris / Black Star
52 Antoine Gyori / Sygma
53 Andrew Reid / Gamma Liaison
54 Art Zamur / Gamma Liaison
55 James Mason / Black Star
56 Tom Stoddart / Katz/Saba
57 Antoine Gyori / Sygma
58 Luc Delahaye / Sipa
60 Corinne Dufka

61 Christopher Morris / Black Star
62 Corinne Dufka
63 Jon Jones / Sygma
64 Luigi Baldelli / Contrasto/Saba
65 Luc Delahaye / Sipa
66 Luc Delahaye / Sipa
67 Tom Haley / Sipa
68 Frank Fournier / Contact
70 Eric Bouvet / Saga
71 Laurent van der Stockt / Gamma Liaison
72 Noel Quidu / Gamma Liaison
74 Patrick Chauvel / Sygma
76 Antoine Gyori / Sygma
77 Ron Haviv / Saba
78 Luc Delahaye / Sipa
80 Peter Northall / AP/Wide World Photos
81 Patrick Durand / Sygma
82 Jon Jones / Sygma
84 Thomas Kern / Lookat
86 Andrew Reid / Gamma Liaison
87 Jon Jones / Sygma
88 Jon Jones / Sygma
90 Tom Haley / Sipa
91 Tom Haley / Sipa
92 Zeljko Maganjic
94 Luc Delahaye / Sipa
96 Luc Delahaye / Sipa
97 Luc Delahaye / Sipa
98 Filip Horvat / Saba
99 Luc Delahaye / Sipa
100 Patrick Chauvel / Sygma
102 Luc Delahaye / Sipa
103 Steve Connors / Select
104 Luc Delahaye / Sipa
106 Tom Haley / Sipa
107 Luc Delahaye / Sipa
108 Antoine Gyori / Sygma
109 Ron Haviv / Saba
110 Luigi Baldelli / Contrasto/Saba
111 Luigi Baldelli / Contrasto/Saba
112 Luc Delahaye / Sipa
114 Gary Knight / Saba
116 Gary Knight / Saba
120 Tom Stoddart / Katz/Saba
126 Eric Bouvet / Saga

Bosnia's Nobel laureate author, Ivo Andric, wrote after World War II: "What a city! Passing away and dying to rise reborn and transfigured."

Eric Bouvet

126

Many of the writers and photographers whose work appears in *Sarajevo* have donated their fees to *Refugees International (RI)*, an independent refugee advocacy organization based in Washington, D.C. *RI* has worked for 14 years to provide a voice for refugees around the world. Following the eruption of fighting in Bosnia, *Refugees International* has been working to mobilize the international community to respond to the humanitarian needs in the former Yugoslavia. *RI* has also played a unique role as adviser on the disbursement of the $50 million Humanitarian Fund for Bosnia-Herzegovina contributed by George Soros. In Sarajevo, Soros-funded projects include providing natural gas heat and other winterization assistance, as well as potable water. "Don't Let Sarajevo Die" has been the theme of *RI's* work; *Sarajevo* is testament to the value of its efforts.

S A R A J E V O

TYPESET IN GILL SANS
USING QUARK XPRESS 3.2 SOFTWARE
ON MACINTOSH COMPUTERS EQUIPPED WITH
SUPERMAC 21-INCH COLOR MONITORS AND
SUPERMAC THUNDER ACCELERATED GRAPHICS CARDS

FINAL LAYOUTS FOR PROOFING PRINTED ON A
SUPERMAC PROOFPOSITIVE DYE SUBLIMATION PRINTER

PHOTOGRAPHIC PRINTS FOR PRODUCTION
BY GRACE ZACCARDI

PRINTED AND BOUND BY AMILCARE PIZZI, MILAN

DATE			